Luster

wesleyan poetry

Luster

Don Bogen

Wesleyan University Press

Middletown, Connecticut

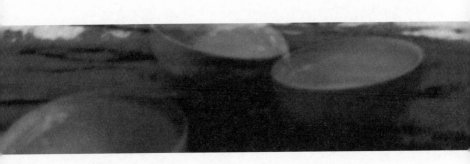

Published by Wesleyan University Press, Middletown, CT 06459

© 2003 by Don Bogen

Printed in the United States of America

5   4   3   2   1

Library of Congress Cataloging-in-Publication Data

Bogen, Don.
 Luster / Don Bogen.
   p. cm. — (Wesleyan poetry)
  ISBN 0-8195-6649-7 (cloth : alk. paper) — ISBN 0-8195-6650-0 (pbk. :
alk. paper)
  I. Title. II. Series.
  PS3552.O4337L87 2003
  811'.54—dc21   2003010105

Interior art, *water5maroon,* by Deborah Brod

For family

In memory of J. H. H. and T. W. L.

Contents

Acknowledgments

Grateful acknowledgment is made to the following journals, in which some of the poems in this book appeared:

Cincinnati Poetry Review: "The Moon in the Water"
Colorado Review: "Coleridge at Midnight," "The Objects"
The Cortland Review: "Stucco"
DoubleTake: "Bullhorn," "The Trains"
Grand Street: "Cardinals"
The Journal: "Rilke in Paris"
Literary Imagination: "Epistle to Dr. Venturo"
The Nation: "Rain Forest"
The New Republic: "The Machines"
The Paris Review: "Thoroughbreds"
Partisan Review: "Bouquinistes"
Prairie Schooner: "La Carte Orange," "The Language," "Métro"
Salmagundi: "Look Out for My Love"
Shenandoah: "One Morning"
Slate: "Meditation on a Line from Whitman"
The Southern California Anthology: "Pedestrian Song"
Stand: "In the Middle of Europe"
Western Humanities Review: "Card Catalog," "Olive"
The Yale Review: "No Friend"

"La Clairière" and "Musée" first appeared in *Poetry* (Modern Poetry Association, 1993).

I am grateful to the Camargo Foundation, the University of Cincinnati Charles Phelps Taft Foundation, the Corporation of Yaddo, and the National Endowment for the Arts for grants that allowed me to complete this book. Special thanks to Cathryn Long, David Rosner, Jason Sommer, and Suzanna Tamminen for their valuable comments and suggestions.

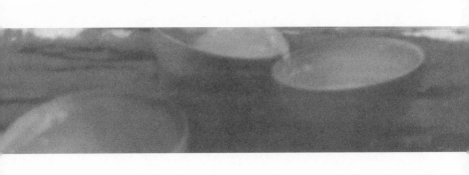

one

Thoroughbreds

Blood flares from the nostrils.
The lungs, the enormous watermelon bellows,
are lined with it.
Legs conduits,
heartstalks that throb with each pulse,
each leap into air and two-beat thump
back on earth.
Their genes are a careful proposition.
They carry their sires like totems
in their names.
Their blood is as stylized as a strut.
Veins push out a nest of tubes to tunnel the meat,
branch like ivy stems beneath the drawn skin.
Nothing in nature reflects their taut poise.

In the boxes,
in the small rings with their necks enclasped by wreaths,
they skitter, coltish, annoyed.
On the track, they glide.
Fluidity comes with their lineage—
training sharpens the point.
In the dust and rumble of the furious brief loop
their purpose may seem blurred.
The curt whip speaks to them.
Their flanks are an argument with friction,
the structure of their haunches
an investment.
Robed in shining blankets,
they wait like fabulous emissaries from another world.
The heart lifts with their promise.
Windows slam at their start.

Bullhorn

A gun
for the mouth.
It sleeps in a drawer,
dangles, ready for work,
off the lead cop's belt
by the nightstick
and black can of mace.
Big metal nipple
with a mesh
you put your lips up to,
wrist strap,
battery in the handle.
Letters felt-tipped
or stenciled on
mark who owns it
and what it will defend.
It clears its throat
with a click,
squawk of
incipient feedback—*You
are in violation* ... Not
a bull's sloppy bellow,
not a horn either,
like that tenor sax
singing under the bridge,
but the dry slap
of authority
claimed from a distance.

At times it seems
a neutral tool,
heroic even, calling out

to the lifeboat
through fog
or reaching up into
a smoldering sixth-floor room.
A searchlight in rubble,
its shout awakes
the nearly dead.
But—*Your attention,*
please—it
always makes you jump:
a warning,
flattened, mechanical,
a half-displayed threat
of force, like
a robot
speaking through
the grille of a truck.
The assistant principal
scouts the halls,
her finger on the trigger.
A crackle—soon
she will get to bark.

Epistle to Dr. Venturo

Throw down your books, you've planned enough for class.
Your students won't be dazzled any less
for time you might spend picking up the news
of happenings where little ever does.
What are friends for? To call you from your work,
recalling friendship with each brief remark,
to fill you in, and fill in the details
of spots unchanged and changes time reveals.
If classic poets, turned away from Rome,
could hold forth on the world from one small farm,
then our provincial outpost might provide
some light—and lines you get to read, not grade.

My theme is cities, how they rise and fall
by laws of nature or by loss of will,
by planning and good sense, or dollars and cents,
by history's dictates or the whims of chance.
Whatever occurred, a city seeking growth
will clean its past and package it as truth.
Take this one: river trade, then pigs, then soap,
a creekbed lined with factories sprouting up,
a booster spirit fattening each year,
dressed now for market in a dream brochure.
Venturo, come discover our new line,
a hint of chic enlarded in each claim.
See Rome on the Ohio, or at least
the San Francisco of the Middle West.

A city does not blossom—it is built.
Its body is geography and wealth.
Where hilltops rise above a sick morass
a city view becomes the best address.

To see, not smell, catch light instead of smog
requires a Jaguar and a Persian rug,
a wine rack, wet bar, shelves of gleaming loot
that complement the claims of real estate.
When cities age, their history grows dear:
the heights become antiques, the pits obscure.
Old names, old top spots in this city's past
are what her newest suitors value most.
Thus *Clifton* (*i.e.*, Cliff-town), *Indian Hill*,
Mt. Airy with its promise never stale,
Heights, Peaks, Runs, Parks, assorted Terraces,
and *Mt. Healthy*, the most ingenuous.
A mountain—or a molehill's—a safe bet:
where burghers feared to tread, the ground was flat.
They left the basin to escape disease;
the new escapees glide by on freeways.
The past lies all before them, where to choose
well tended slopes that help investments rise.

Now let's descend for local atmosphere.
Breathe deeply. There is something in the air.
It drifts through ozone, floating on a breeze
of hydrocarbons, mist, suspended grease,
past rib pits, rusting playgrounds, parking lots,
a scabrous billboard hawking cigarettes,
Chevies on blocks, one skittering brown dog,
street kids, and drunks awake enough to beg.
Collected, dense, familiar, it will rise
into the convolutions of the nose,
then drop, then spread out as it speeds along
to graze the fragile blossoms of each lung
and ride the blood until it finds its own
niche in the chemical storeroom of the brain.
Thus great *Pollution* sweeps past every eye
to stir the heart and take our breath away.

But stay downtown, Venturo, and look up
where tax abatements gather all our hope.
As aging streets, like bodies, thrive or rot,
some buildings fall—and some rejuvenate.
A tenement turns condo, news reports—
and tenants load their goods in shopping carts.
A wall is stripped, fine plasterwork revealed,
officials paid off, old contracts annulled,
old ceilings shown, old residents shown out,
floors newly sanded and new closings set.
While gilded doormen scan the lowering street,
art-deco elevators trace the height,
the broadening suites, the dear amenities
expanding as the asking prices rise
till at the top, glassed, staring at the sun,
gleam pools, a jogging track and health salon.
The ski machines, the splendid rowers shine,
and sweat glows like a polish on each tan.
What's steep stays clean. A rich aerobic food
scours the narrow passageways of blood,
beats back the years, builds confidence anew
and helps the highest ever still to grow.
A city learns to lift its searching eyes
and tune its voices upward into praise:
O brave repurchased Eden, looming clear,
cloud-spanning aerie, palace of pure air,
where bright, forever young, gods of the hill
may sport at their own sweet will!

Cocktail Party, 1953

And the Republic summons Ike,
the mausoleum in her heart.

Zero hour—he pours.
Wet fire splits night from day,
a ribbon of red gold
cutting its road again
between the hills of ice:
white blocks, then chunks of glass
with little cracks, at last
amorphous rounded lumps
slippery, voluble.
Now he loosens his tie
and paces among the suits
and stiff bras, past the buffet,
the ash trays on chair arms
and end tables, blurred drops
spattered across blond curves.
His brain is a jewel in flames
revolving, pulsing light
long after the nation's asleep.
His heart is an underground test,
his drink missile fuel.
Ideas flare through the rooms
like meteors above
the luminous city below.
That critic slashing air,
historian on the rise,
hot editor, the host
of a dozen scenes like this—
he moves from star to star,
the fever of their talk

simmering his dreams.
Cold-war ambitions flit
among the gossip and smoke,
the snack cart, the help,
a wife set off on the couch
like a glazed tulip.
The best minds of an age
are sparring here. Aglow
inside the brilliant ring,
he rattles ice and starts
his preemptive strike of wit.
No need—she shows her hand:
a melting stare, plump lips
burnished gleaming red,
the chalice of her dress
where he would sip.

The Moon in the Water

How can a guy climb trees, say, "Me Tarzan, you
Jane," and make a million? It was like stealing.

That man jogging half-naked through the arboretum
is the relic of an Olympic swimming star.
His amplified yowl swings through arroyos of yucca
like a demented cry of triumph or a curse.
Rich, flat, comfortable in black and white,
he poses before invisible charging rhinos, talks to chimps,
and seems a bit lost in his voluminously stylish suit
when he dines at the Brown Derby after work.

He is not, after all, the articulate slumming aristocrat
of the books. His character's a sack of air,
and the pidgin English he is made to blurt nails him
to a cliché. The bad natives, all spidery body paint
and dangling skulls, are undoubtedly more civilized—
hence corrupt. On the other side, he is elevated
above those good but dumb packbearers
by his instinctual cunning and astounding white skin.

In the tank scenes he resembles a furless otter
and is most at home. Frolicking with Boy
or miming a furious breast stroke with a knife between his teeth,
he looks as if he could hold his breath forever.
His sleek thighs glisten among the treasure chests
and drugged alligators. His feet seem webbed.
Free inside the glass-walled river, he is able to transform sport
into his own kind of performing art.

When he breaks the surface and crawls to some convenient rocks
there is a moment of primitive beefcake he has to enjoy.
Then Jane calls. The soggy domestic comedy of a jungle bungalow:

servants monkeying around, minor annoyances at mealtimes,
and today problems with the vine-and-pulley dumbwaiters
that make the whole house work. *Ungawa!* he sputters
at the pygmy elephant tangled in his bamboo harness,
Ungawa!—a frustrated husband blowing his top.

These carefully rehearsed explosions titillate:
eyes a charming smolder, hands caught in a half-clench—
then at last the relief of a long dream swing
across the processed screen. Tension and release, confinement
and escape. But the main theme is greed.
Ambitious Cockneys, spider women and proto-Nazis
scramble for the rhinestone in a plaster idol's eye,
then fall off cliffs or get swallowed in the ubiquitous quicksand

again and again. Old Janes and Boys gone whiskery circle his chest
like asteroids. A slough of Wagneroid mood music muddies
his classic lines. In the hectic late films he finds himself drawn
to the opulent simplicity of the elephants' graveyard.
When they take him at last like King Kong to the big city,
he responds with a thirty-five-second swan dive off the Brooklyn
    Bridge.
Watch now: his street clothes are sinking in the East River,
his pale arm arcs like a slice of moon.

The Trains

Old closed-down schools. Hardly monuments,
these chipped limestone and scaly brick eyesores
loom over their asphalt lots like dinosaurs
in tar pits. An air of squat self-importance
still wraps them in its bad smell. Their doors
festooned with oversized padlocks, chain-link fence
girding a down-at-heels magnificence,
they look as if they expected something more.

What could they want? Their teeming century
built them to resemble overgrown ruins—
and now that's what they are. The flood of children
who filled their castle gates and galleries
with whispers, shrieks, and babble is a thin
murmur in the suburbs. Their dignity
erodes like those stolid nonentities
whose names snooze over porticos in the sun.

Harrison, McKinley, U. S. Grant—
how have the mighty fallen? The busts and portraits,
even the doilies with their silhouettes
have left the halls. Face down, the President
presides in the attic near a cabinet
of stacked, decaying readers. Curled and faint
history lessons yellow toward parchment
on open shelves. School boards meet in chests.

Beneath a still unfashionable ceiling fan
order reigns at last in the classroom.
No talking now, no straining hands, no problems
on the blackboard. Clamped to their rails, four trains

of oak and wrought iron desks align the gloom.
Who would have thought this was their destination?
It's sad how long these neat rows have retained
the threadbare certainties that bolstered them.

Card Catalog

I love the gargantuan simplicity of the thing:
a piece of furniture with a whole room built around it,
fat as an ocean liner, obsolescent as a department store,
massive and layered like a vast apartment complex twenty floors high.

The drawers are a study in multiplicity,
each nearly identical but for the odd nick or stain,
the calm grained surfaces darkening variously with the years
and the different amounts of light passing down from high windows.
Each has its little plate, its round pull like a doorknob—
Knock, knock. Who's there? The residents keep changing,
but they all have exotic names like Abs-Axi or Rib-Rica.
They get a lot of mail, all postcards.

Such ponderous decorum. The sheer bulk of the whole
settles into even its smallest parts:
wood boxes in wood troughs that drag and creak as you tug at them,
as if to remind you that this is all hard work,
the drawer impossible to balance in one hand, the clunky pull-out shelves
clattering as the box is shoved onto them,
stiff white cards and a brass rod to anchor each stack.

Once you're finally set up, a fluid ease comes in.
I like to dabble with my fingers.
Flip, flip—titles flicker across my eyes,
registering, filing, cross-referencing, replicating and hiding themselves
in the swampy catalog of my head.
I wish I had a memory this clean!
Still, I make the most of the journey,
the numbers and letters like roadsigns decorating the corners,
the special directions in red—*See also, See under*—that can lead you
    almost anywhere,

mysterious bibliographic abbreviations, hand-printed lists of years on a
    periodical card
fading back from felt-tip to ballpoint to fountain pen.

Each card has its story:
some dog-eared, ripped or smudged with thumbprints,
others so pristine I want to skirt around them delicately
so as not to wake them up.
When I come across, as if by accident, a card with my own name on it,
I feel a kind of embarrassed responsibility,
as if I'd stumbled on a snow-covered plot of ground I inherited years ago
and now am obliged to tend.

At the terminal, of course, I can see my name in lights,
and I admit the whole system is closer to a brain,
with its minuscule interlocking channels, electrical streams and
    diversions,
its choices, random searches and dark stretches of being down.
Besides, you get to sit with it, you can talk to it over the phone.
It tries, I know, to be user-friendly, while the catalog prefers to use *you*.

But even as I process these words, memory rebels
and brings back all the different halls of cabinets where I've worked:
a pseudo-Gothic chapel, a mausoleum full of drawers,
a hexagon enclosing a busy hive of stacks—
settings pulled out for a moment as if in a wood box themselves.
Seattle: *See also* Drizzle, Roethke, Salmon. Berkeley: *See* Eucalyptus,
    Josephine Miles.

two

Etudes

Métro

Through tunnels, on walkways, up and down stairs,
past the curt announcement of the warning horn, two-step swish of doors
and rubber gliding over the rails,
among the swirled currents of sweat and perfumes, the press of skin
shifting against cotton, linen, nylon, warmth and respiration—
and above all this, like orchids floating on a stream,
the delicate, infinitely varied faces,
wearing some worry now, half-reposed in reading
or settling themselves to the prospects of the day—
each morning in this lit room speeding and slowing in the dark,
among the fashionable ads and clamorous graffiti,
the eyes with their questions too direct and too subtle for speech,
holding the language like a new taste in my mouth,
I was carried along, part of it all and set apart.

The Language

At the end of the day I felt how my face had been wearing the language—
not like a garment but inside, a posture,
my lips drawn outward to caress a vowel, my tongue
distinctly tapping the palate for one consonant
while another arose like a faint growl back in the throat,
all the hidden muscles stretched or contracted in new ways
to build a pose for the jaw and cheekbones, an attitude
defined by the pulse of deliberate attention that would extend
to the eyes as they narrowed to catch movements of lips,
the ears alert for every soft word,
the tilt of my head, shoulders angled forward,
my whole bearing set to bring life closer in a crowded café.

Musée

In this calm world I love,
among the perfected arrangements gathered on the walls—
portraits of royals and merchants, allegorical spectacles,
café crowds, pondscapes, bowls of fruit—
I found myself yearning for the awkwardness of talk,
its gaps and misstatements, the way over time it goes somewhere
you never expected, lifting the heart or dropping us into darkness.
Here and not here, you were a brush of cloud, a blue scarf
defining the moment around it, language in my lips and tongue
quick before it dries on the illegible stamped card.

Bouquinistes

Old prints and books, old medals, buttons, sepia postcards—
I admired the compact abundance,
the invisible careful choices that made it all seem rich,
the ingenious green wooden stands themselves
set apart yet open to the street, the trees and the river.
Living in two worlds, I was drawn to the freedom of this browsing,
its small bright discoveries within the dailiness of the setting.
There are books I wanted to enter just for the sense
of being lost in them yet still aware of a breeze in the chestnut,
my thoughts of you, the river, its currents, islands, where the bridges are.

La Carte Orange

Like everything flat or caught in time, I look awkward
cramped in the photo-booth picture on the upper right,
scowling, it seems, at the thicket of numbers and directions,
the rim of the official stamp staining my black-and-white shoulder,
and the slick little pocket for the weekly Métro ticket
that would pass in and out, in and out,
gracing my days with its ease,
giving each one a shape, if I can follow it,
that was gliding, fluid, effortless and clear.

La Clairière

In memory I know even the clatter of small white cups on their saucers,
the hurried cube of sugar and the ordinary spoon
will matter. The copper-colored bar will gleam
and the street outside beyond the plate-glass wall,
a trough of shade between gray nineteenth-century buildings,
will break into light. The moment will open with the same fresh promise
streaming from the two spouts of the espresso machine,
the gurgling pipe of steamed milk shouting to the day,
huddled conversations—hellos, good-byes—as morning sweeps us on,
the warm cup balanced in my thumb and forefinger
and the taste, direct and supple, deepening with the will
to meet the day in its changes, not to arrange, fix or clarify
but to spend, even now, what memory would hoard.

Rilke in Paris

Du mußt dein Leben ändern

Elegance of streets and squares,
this café or that,
a shaded wall, a demure zoo
where a panther paced behind railings
in his barred pavilion.

Paced—or posed? It was like that:
fin de siècle cage on its pedestal
set up like a sculptor's
and the poet impossible not to imagine there,
motionless, staring,
till the one picture enters the heart
and stops.

The city still presents
its quick tableaux:
shutters thrown open above a boulevard,
or one of the old ones, as he called them,
approaching down a narrow lane.
I have a little gift for you, she said,
as I watched through a screen of lines.

To think of him seeing all this and walking past,
the rhythm of the language in his mind
self-enclosed, as I imagine it,
thickening, hidden
like a childhood ritual, a secret dance.
And later at a table under darkening eaves,
something finally set down.

Dawn landscape
of slate and chimney pots, invisible bells,
invisible heels on cobblestones—
a descent, then, to enter this world.
Walking past book stalls just opening,
the day's flowers in buckets.

In the museum, a stone garden.
Bone-smooth torsos, a hand propped on sticks—
fragments of the gods
without their makers.
They stare. They have demands
he began to hear, after a long time,
as light.

Beauty
that blinds.
There is a stillness he saw
inside everything, and it ripens
till the street outside the window be mute,
the flutter of a leaf caught
precisely in the picture.

Coleridge at Midnight

Frost on the child's face,
a tincture clouding the glass.

You, a swirl, suddenly *there* in the oral exam,
as if it were a séance.

We were discussing anecdotes—
the obliterating energy that sent you weaving
from side to side of the road,
your unending monologue a flower blooming from a flower
from a flower as the listener trailed behind—
the exam itself at that moment
a celebration of the whirling light
your skull held.

It was as if your mind had ramified
into snowflakes falling all around us,
and we'd pause to stare at one or another
before they melted in our palms.

All this beauty we have made from your failure.

I thought of you holding forth in your rooms at Göttingen
as drifts quieted the streets.
Lovely dark world of candles and sleighs
with a voice keeping it alive.

Your living voice is ink.
How you spoke to the child in a prayer,
kept praising the friend, hinted painfully
to a woman who was never allowed to listen—

no one more domestic than you
or more lost.

These one-way conversations in blank verse,
blessings poured out from some bones.

I had a cold and I took a remedy.
It led me beside the deepening piles of foolscap
and gave no relief.
Writing this, I was interrupted.

The exam is a conversation
from which I drop away.

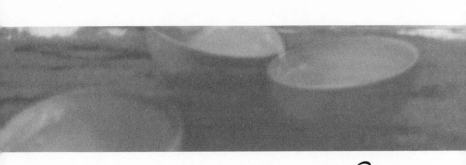

three

In the Middle of Europe

We walked along the wall by the Bismarck lodging,
a round stone hut with a conical hat and windows,
and I thought of the man there in his Romantic student days
(as Romantic as I hoped mine would be) perched over the river
like a watchman on this overgrown, half-vanished ridge
between the Middle Ages and the train station.
Göttingen was gray brick against snow,
pure Gothic aspiration and student life in cellars:
clubs, songs, Latin, mugs and scars.
We walked past cindery backlots of houses
where the town's poor (mostly Turks and Serbs then)
ate potatoes all winter, the limits of life
settling down on them like a quilt of sludgy soot.

Twenty years. I remember the Bismarck Tower
and how I could never find it when I wandered in the woods
alone like the sad hero of a Schubert song
I didn't know about then, the words so earnest and thin
a tenor could overpower them, were it not
for the fat prop of piano. All that yearning
and key changes, diminuendo snapped
by a sudden resolution. There was a fortified border
near where we were walking. The war in Asia
and the draft which fueled it weighed down every small decision.
My life was a tissue of "if"s. Its progress depended
on scholarships, on what I thought you might do or say,
on a lottery of birthdates.

I'm glad that's over. And now the border's gone,
with its lies and watchtowers. Those shaggy students
trying to look like us, like all of us then,
who offered to buy my shoes and jeans on the side streets

of East Berlin are probably parents now. They want
a car that doesn't stink, they want to be able
to take their kids to a theme park. And if
they have to fight for the jobs *Gastarbeiter* once had,
if their clothes and accents mark them
as provincial, lazy, a drain on the Bundesbank,
that is how the limits of their lives are changed.

There were smaller changes then, though they seemed
momentous. I remember wanting to tell you
about Willy Brandt—how startling it was, purifying even,
to see a man who had "betrayed the Fatherland"
(the opposition highlighted his work in the Resistance)
elected Chancellor. It was like the days I would wake up
to find new snow covering the whole long view from my window,
the lack of shape or color, the sheer boundlessness of the scene
a silent promise. I loved that kind of moment,
a choice or a perspective suddenly slicing life clean
from history, the wanderer poised at the edge
of the forest path, lake or mountain peak,
tasting the new world in his lungs, ready to sing.

Those twenty-year-old skinheads in the photograph taken near Leipzig
weren't singing but cheering, their arms raised in salutes
I used to see only in films. Does everything
come back? They had just driven out the foreigners,
Vietnamese this time, from a hostel. Their heads blunt
as sharks', the gash of their grins terrifying,
but still in their confident eyes a familiar element:
that exuberance—even in the photo you can see it
brimming their skulls, pulsing among them like a charge—
a radiant solidarity stuffing the heart so full
it grows beyond limits. Energy, unity, getting yourself
"together," as we put it—I thought of it all

as an affirmation of life, for you embodied
in a much-treasured, child-like social enthusiasm,
for me only possible in pure solitary moments
with snow coming down in the middle of Europe.

Our walk was a series of jagged disagreements,
small dissonances linking into icy crescendos
that scarred the air. You took the high ground
of complete spontaneity, a fortress of delight
from which my own self-consciousness had excluded me—
I could be free if I let myself, nothing had changed,
it was all as simple as a song. (And there were plenty of songs
we both knew that showed the way.) I know I wanted you,
but my desire kept slipping off into a broader realm
that was finally just dream. There was something virginal
behind it all—our music, our faith in hitchhiking,
even our hashpipes and all-night giggling—
as we turned away from the mad, impossible world.
It was as if we were citizens of a country
that had always existed but was not yet recognized,
all of us coming together in a borderless allegiance
and a yearning, blind as a lost child's love.

We circled the core of the city, its medieval heart
the wall had been constructed to protect:
town square and goose-girl fountain, Ratskeller,
spires poking the sky. For Bismarck the wall
was already just a walking path—not a boundary
but a shortcut home from school. The world he saw
was full of decaying borders, arcane
and tenuous as the outlines on a map. You could
cut through them if you had the will. Your yearning,
aged and disciplined to a kind of dense purity,
could reach to the edge of Paris.

In Göttingen I was stiff and hollow, a thin bronze bell
without a tongue—such were *die Leiden meines Wanderjahrs.*
It seems to me now that my sorrow and loaded silences
fed not only on the inevitable differences between us
but on the language that was gradually
finding its home in my mouth: the blood-and-iron
set of the jaw, clauses like a list of demands
while the main verbs waited, heavy with prefixes—
everything in abeyance, suspended like a sword
that would finally drop and make it all come clear.
You said I had grown prematurely old.
It's true I was ossified—not in the habits of age
but in a rigid adolescence, in dreams and grievances
pushed up against a wall. Boundaries—I wanted them all
to vanish. There was sleet in the air.
The scarf you'd made for me froze and thawed, froze and thawed
in my breath. I remember complaining
that the cold had made you brittle,
but you were far beyond the argument, bundled
in your own concerns, out of reach by then.

Look Out for My Love

Or that we would want to be Indians or maybe
clichés of our grandparents with tiny
wire-rimmed spectacles and feathery hair, or a spaceship
would come down and swoop us away to a new world that was really
an old world reclaimed, purified, Atlantis—Hail Atlantis!

or that chemicals could save us

or love, as if we understood
its intricate hooks and eyes, the way it is not at last
the wave or even the froth but what's left in
the waiting pools: pocked shells, fronds, multicolored
clamps and suckers of all sorts, clinging and fluttery or
at rest calmly filtering for nourishment, for breath

or the earth—how we loved her—would sustain us with its
bok choy grown in the mud of vacant lots by lean-to shanties,
its stumpy carrots, strung beans and ubiquitous saw-toothed dope

or the red star of the East rising, our lapel cameos
of gleaming Lenin, goateed oracular Trotsky or—take
your pick—a closed fist, a leaf, a yellow
submarine surfacing with a peace sign jutting from the bridge

This smorgasbord of past fantasies,
this rummage heap of elaborate masks and blindfolds,
this patchwork of tatters so variegated it hangs on,
even now, in a rag bag of nostalgia

or stringing beads on fishing line, facets of colored glass
filling endless tiny hours, brocading bell bottoms, body painting
in ecstatic parks, blown roses or fat paisley scrolls
on the great rolled collars of adornment

or Blake or Yeats, the gyres on our sweatshirts,
the progress of our characters through time on the phases
of the moon, our parables of reversal, our folk tales
with their predictable happy surprises—everyone is susceptible,
everyone is the birthday boy

or—if they would only listen—our music in its dead-step blues
and endlessly elaborated distortion, our light shows
squeezed from tubes—if they would only listen, if they would only
light up—and they did, villages blazing before the stoned eyes
of our doubles with their hootches, M-16s and Bics

or that we could dance the night away

or that we could make the perfect gesture, nominate
an appropriate pig for President, play theater in a courtroom,
choreograph messages as devious and self-engrossing
as a circuit board

This redundant self-canceling technology, this riotous Victoriana
reproduced on bedspreads, these Pre-Raphaelite blank-eyed
wantons alluring in patchouli, our hands amazed all over them,
scarcely connected to our shoulders

or fat candles guttering in a garage room where they
are casting your chart, finding the trines and oppositions, rifling
the mystic East, runes, Egypt, Gregorian chant or
Stockhausen on the deafening earphones, your days, loves,
death even laid out on the wheel

or shaman lecturers, groove-on T.A.'s in their turtlenecks
and minis, discussions in an oak grove, by a fountain, in a dorm room or
the kindly professor's pipe-scented book-lined office, turn
to page 417, dear ones, and tell me now what is life

or hate your father, love your mother

or marching, shouting, sitting down and standing
up for your right to speak, to mill before a line
of unsheathed bayonets, your right not to be blown into
a porcupine of shrapnel or to have to wrap yourself in tinfoil or pretend
you think you're a car for six weeks in basic training

or the glee he felt, gyrating like a crankshaft
in the smoky closet, sparking off mad puns or later in the metal bed
an intricate plan to end the war which he knew he said made
no sense but still had to be worked out day after day,
a spider's web churning in blank light

This—dig it—homage to the oppressed,
jailbird entrepreneurs haranguing under the free sun,
their whittled slang, pauses and iconic postures as in photographs

with a rifle and beret, a wicker throne, a feathered spear,
their cellblock Marxism and dark vanguard scars

or that we were the masses, there were so many of us,
flooding the plaza then the streets like canals
between the closed-up shops, miles from the war plants
and dying warehouses, the slums walled off by the town's definition,
the unspeakable stupefied suburbs we'd all been allowed to escape

or ascending the Rapunzel-tower dorms, with their sign-outs, suicide
    windows
and three feet on the floor, cleaning big stew pots in the co-ed
co-ops, in communes of all kinds—crash pad,
mini-frat house, love nest, party cell—in cinder-block
villages managed by agencies, your grandfather's brown-shingle mansion
split into a dozen flats

or they said it was impossible for a man to live and breathe
underwater and we knew, our rippled bodies swaying like seaplants
in the dim hall by the stacked amps and feedback, we knew
they were wrong

or daisies slipped into rifle barrels, the orchid framed in hair
above an ear, tongued, drooping lilies, piles of frangipani nestled
at the guru's muslin knees—orange, mauve and scarlet, all the insides
pushed out, sweet traps hiding nothing, giving off
honey to the air

or the Little Prince, his friendly serpent and mystical lesson of flight

This travelling, by thumb in the backs of deux chevaux,
cross-country mattress-sided microbuses, even the odd
semi, these flowered jeans in the airport, vinyl backpacks
flying through the sky, these jungle boats, stretch helicopters, hovercraft
peripatetic and relentless

or the number you'd discover if you could figure out
the code on the album cover among the stars, the rainbow
and goofy animal costumes, and when you called it they would come
from wherever they were in the world because they could tell
you were one of the special ones who'd know they were coming—*Please
    don't*
be long—coming to take you away

or dead stars, the huge dark implosions,
three on one late-summer day

or riding like a rabbit in the belly of the nation,
our demographic lumpishness—engulfed, shifting, protuberant,
poking the muscled walls with our big ears and feet, fur and bone
nearly indigestible, a blob in the tube
suffusing into nutrients as the beast sleeps

or the sun refuse to shine

The Objects

These objects that come when I call but never speak.

A milkshake glass, hooded sweatshirt, hand-made paperweight
lonely among garrulous memories.

They cut out a hole around them like a man in a white field,
a man behind the wheel of a car.

Because they are piled up they are disconnected.
Because they are solid they seem unreal.
Artifacts gathered for the journey
near the scarabs and terra cotta jars.

Old toys, photographs
family stories have chattered into silhouettes—
a clutter of things that will survive me
turns away

dragging a little scar across the past.

No Friend

A couple with their
changing friends, the ease
of that closeness

I envy—why
do they let me see
again and again

this pattern of love
and betrayal? In the little
intimacies shared quickly

and the hearty swoops soon after,
seeds of his father's drunk
reversals, her mother's

faceted bitterness.
A quartet, then, scored
to build and explode.

After the crescendo,
fizzled echoes of themes
grown familiar, a coda

like a sudden blossom
where the new players' tones
don't fit: garish,

discordant, insane,
as it turns out again.
I watch the flare

and slow fade, like novae
in the old constellations.
So many women,

fragile, gone hysterical,
so many brooding men
who would "lash out"—

over and over
they sink into cliché
and flail as they go down.

Silence, then a splinter
of rage. In the sad
dark, awkward, I

listen, no friend.

four

Five Runs in France

Soulangis

Silence of wheat, sunflower rustle,
    then another grove—
gliding along groomed paths
    among ferns and chartreuse slugs,
damp earth smell, damp air
    and out to open sun—
a white glint, yellow, then green again
    striping the afternoon.

Kerizac

Half-clear, no, foggy
or one clump of cloud black with the sun behind it.
Stone farms' crumbling fences,
mud, smoke, chickens, damp sheep.
In the sea wind from far off, sheets flap on a line.
The shape of breathing traces each dip and rise
around hillocks and fast small streams,
moss on a signpost, a stroke of wet light.

Flumet

Cold mist, frost on dead grass.
First breaths jagged glass, pushed out white.
Switchbacks cut the long slow climb
past ski-lift pylons, empty stations,
villages jumbled at the feet of chapels,

their gravestones thrown back by the frozen ground.
Runnels in sunlight still dripping through tubes of ice.
On the highest peaks, just snow.

Cassis

Each step up among burnt trunks and scrub lifts dust,
pebbles that stream back down,
echoes under magpies' caws.
A ladder of air shoves open the lungs,
deepens a gaze toward the horizon.
Landmarks, surprises: that boulder at the curve—
    a lizard sunning on it—sharp thyme smell,
first turn, first sight of the sea.

Le Champ-de-Mars

A closed pet store, a square
    asleep in summer trees,
wall of apartments with no one home
    surveying the field and its circuit:
this loop of time in gravel, clack
    of boule balls, bus exhaust,
flutter of languages thick near the tower
    fading to breath and footfall.

Olive

You see them on hillsides
or lining the roads through vineyards
like a parade of sun-gnarled field hands
called out for the master's return.
Working trees, they all look heavy with domesticity,
even the single one here in the garden
holding up a spidery net of shade for us.

In an orchard it would be cropped and sprayed,
thickened with needs that plump to harvest.
But here it pushes out inaccessible tentacles,
its high limbs narrow as vines dangling streamers.
The trunk, iron-hard and barely broader than a wrist,
sways, wobbling the entire apparatus
like an oversized umbrella full of holes.

Ludicrous, yes—but what history:
presses of wood and stone,
terra cotta amphorae loaded on racks in the holds—
the ship of work passing year after year
into the harbor of taste.
My tongue is anointed,
my brain is a rubbed lamp swirling with tales.

I remember an olive-wood cane
older than the woman who used it,
the grace of its darkened handle, curve of its grain
where a branch kept turning toward the light.
The craftsman must have spent weeks approaching it,
shaping, polishing, calling it out,
his hand on every surface.

But this one is untouched—
all free spindliness in the wind.
Pocked fruit drops like an afterthought.
The tree whistles
in its corner of the garden,
a slow investment in dirt, rain and blunt reliable sun
whose only return is survival.

Rain Forest

Olympic Peninsula

No lianas, no
chattering rufous monkeys, no
bird cries even, under
the canopy of firs.
Clouds you can't see
filter the shadows.
The air is dense
with intricate
respiration: sacs and
pores, the transaction
of gasses in half-light.
Rain a scrim.

Everything falls,
dripping a blurred
hush. Innumerable
whispers in the sodden
duff: mosses, flakes
of bark, black twigs soft
as noodles. A poor soil
where life does its work.
So the dropped limb slowly
fills with its own dust,
a cracked urn sinking
in fungal growth.

Curds, clumps, fleshy
congealed waves—they
feed on rot. If you
touched them, they would
crumble. If you knelt down

or stumbled on a damp root,
you would be covered,
the world glazed and
layered: debris, and ferns,
and high up in the limbs still
standing, flowering vines
dangling their speechless heads.

Cardinals

Just before daybreak
    tweezering at the cold edge
for a disk of sun.

Whipping, whipping air
    out from the poplar in waves:
Here I am, here, here.

Common, loud, garish,
    a pinup in the field guide,
amateurs' first crush.

Flitting jerky-hop
    from twig to twig on the limb—
never the right spot.

A shopkeeper's eye,
    relentless, shutter-quick, honed
on the day's small gains.

Perched on the phonelines
    calling sunset, hooked around
the black rope of talk.

One Morning

Light playing on the surfaces of two walls—
buff stucco planes and the angle between them,
their shades warming and cooling as clouds clump, pass and thin:
gray-brown and manila-brown, white
coffee and English tea, skin tones
on either side of a tan line that deepens and fades.

Who could hold on to these colors?
I think of the ridiculous names on paint strips—
antler, cinnamon, adobe, Taos dawn—
that someone has to make up each year for the new combinations of
     pigment,
how they all dissolve finally into mere sensation or sentiment,
unable to define, able at best only to evoke—
and what they evoke is gone even before the names are chosen.

Try metaphors: morning as a ballet,
dense, polyrhythmic, all beams and spots,
the action shifting upstage and down as light constructs the texture,
sudden washes sweeping across the walls like curtains or weather.
Or morning as a weather report,
the meteorologist frantically trying to interpret and predict
while the screen keeps changing behind his back.

I'd like to get beyond words for once.
I'd like not to reflect on but just reflect what's in front of me,
myself a surface, like a polished mirror
or a pair of eyes without the brain attached.
Language can feel like a clot in the flow of seeing,
jumbled, intransigent, an abandoned beaver dam
diverting and half-clogging the inexhaustible whitewater stream.

Light drifts, pools, skitters, rushes, eddies, filters through a haze,
stirring up so much intricacy it spills into simplification—
this morning two walls, sun and clouds are more than enough.

From a Daybook

Cassis, 1992–1993

Three steps of a dove's cry from a dark space in the pine—
hoo-hoo-*hoo*!—breathy, rasping, a flutter in the throat
at dawn. Call, pause and repeat—hoo-
hoo-*hoo*!—arranging the silence around it.

Working on a terrace overlooking a garden
overlooking the sea, time in the church bells,
or more subtly in the awning I keep having to extend,
a sweatshirt discarded mid-morning.
Dry light's a tease.
It massages my forearm, glints off a blank page,
peeks over the awning's scalloped edge.
It invites me to work outside all day
as at a café table, absorbing its warmth and release,
hiding from its glare.

Three notes of the church bell fading over and over.
They are carting a box up the narrow street,
through gates, down into a house of dirt.
When it is settled and covered,
friends move off in stiff clumps and nervous black cars,
pain gradually letting go the backs of their throats as speech begins
to deliver the body into memory,
the bell marking the process over and over
while the sun peaks, mourners go somewhere to eat,
and the beloved drifts in their changing words.

This small ocean, the middle of a world,
old ports rising and falling with the swells of commerce,

their long streets reeling languages on the way to the harbor—
the Ramblas, Cours Saleya, the Canebière—
gull shrieks, slosh and thunk of the waking market,
its first cries, slip-flop of fish, shells tumbling onto plywood
as light pries open its districts block by block.

To know that shadow is the servant of light
and speech the servant of air
and art failure, failure—nothing is held.
To know that the painter staring at these dry hills
dotted with clumps of scrub oak and stubbly broom
worked over and over to bring out shapes
the sun might define for an hour one afternoon
and left them like memories in the beautiful lie of his colors.

Ropes rattling against hollow masts in the port,
a muted thudding, a clank when a pulley or hook hits the pole,
rising above the undertones of creaking, lapping and rocking—
waves on stones, hulls against rubber tires on the pilings—
the Mistral ferrying its brown smell of burning vines,
a winter music sweeping out to sea.

Futile to fix this morning on paper—
gusts of salt air and a thin fog riding in.
Futile to feed memory what I think it will want—
let it wander and make things up.
Rustling shade from the parasol pine, brief whitecaps,
calls from small boats lofting or lost in swept light—
futile to want any of this fixed,
to hold, as the breezes keep pushing in,
a moment when I'm not here.

Stucco

Morning sky, the San Gabriels amazingly visible:
eggplant and faded butter tones lumping on the horizon,
the pale khaki dot of a yucca and, higher,
a green line of scraggly firs.

Palms parade down the foothills.
Then the short, tough grasses—hybrid, exotic,
defining empty lawns.

Wide streets sleeping in.
Walkways curve among the rosebushes.

These bungalows bleaching for seventy years:
round arches, porches designed for awnings no longer there.
In the foot-thick stucco walls
a blunt hint of adobe anchors the revival.

Always this nod to a mythic past.
Thin dreams of realtors
inscribed in the layered crust.

Light streams and wavers,
all the smooth cream-colored surfaces mottled and pitted.

A certain broad dryness is spreading in the sun,
capacious, democratic and matte.

Meditation on a Line from Whitman

They are so lonely, our dying cities,
specks on the vast familiar map that looks like a side of beef,
in boldface or marked with a circled dot,
ringed by their beltways, linked into nameless constellations by the
    interstates.
Some are red giants, expanding and cooling in the smoggy dusk,
others dwarfs with dense shrunken cores
or pulsars throbbing out their last light.

On my way out of town, I drive through a fold in time,
a tunnel through the history of shopping:
boarded-up storefronts on the narrow commercial streets,
the old strips and plazas with a muffler shop or a chicken fryer left,
and larger sites—a five-and-dime blown out into a warehouse,
fast-food shops, all local chains now,
with their scratchy speakers and pot-holed drive-thru lanes;
then the first real malls, big as aircraft carriers, low and blocky,
their outlying coffee shops and two-screen theaters like escorts;
at last a quieting stretch, the freeway growing walls
and the walled tracts all around nestled in their names—
The Willows, Hunt Club Crossing, Hidden Acres—
their malls planted, soft-colored, smoothly designed,
broad single lumps surrounded by asphalt prairie,
distant and unobtrusive as buttes.

What is an executive home? Who lives there?
I imagine the orbiting managers, shifted every five years
to another desirable location beyond the beltway,
another stand of young pines and curving roads, another commute,
another city as a set of season tickets to the football games
or a pass even to skyboxes if they should rise so high.
Some will. At home, in their brief stops,

they glide effortlessly up the ladder of good schools,
ladder of yard space, of techno-buttons
in the family room, vehicles lined on the drive,
the whole ensemble an island slipping further and further from the
    rotted core.

Bland wealth of the suburbs,
it's useless to keep despising it, I know,
unfair to friends who have to live there—or else in slums—
but sometimes its cultivated innocence feels like an assault.
I don't want to join the country club because there are no parks.
I don't want to leave my car in an underground garage,
rise to the office, sink at the end of day,
drive home unable to stop or roll down the windows
till I see the familiar guard in his gatepost waiting at the start of our
    street.

This sealed-off life—
even the ease of it disturbs me.
Secure, imperturbable, it floats in a daydream of possibilities—
a trip to the water park, things to buy at the hardware depot,
quality time, preparation for success,
Have you outstript the rest? Are you the President?—
a huge ball of dust drifting and whirling
as the light from burnt-out stars races over it.

Pedestrian Song

Eyes behind car windows
don't want to see you.
Lungs don't breathe your air.
The head a bland globe
in the glare of glass,
neck a stick, spine a stick,
limbs four sticks tipped
in pads, rods and hooks
to press, twist, swivel.
Crab in the shell,
pale brain in the skull,
that wriggling thing cased
in bright metal follows
the lights twelve feet up,
out of this world.
Where is it going
in its carton of steel,
the body transformed
to a blunt dream?
It shines in the dark:
high beam, low beam
nosing a course
focused as a shark's
through a shipwreck—
you can't predict it.
The signs flash clear—
Don't Walk, Don't Walk—
you can smell the heat
from their hoods, you can hear
valves snapping as they wait
along the faint line

that keeps you safe.
Oh, you are soft,
tiny as a rabbit,
your only defense
a tissue of faith.
Stay quick, then. If you think
there's a person in there,
look again, think back
to your own long spin:
secure, controlled,
in touch with the wheel—
then reeling and screeching
till at last you can stop
and the whole world starts up around you.

five

The Machines

There is the romance of naive technology
in the tree itself. Though it's hardly a machine,
the looped cords, alligator clips and sockets festooning it
add to the exotic glimmer of shaggy nature set inside.
In pockets of shadow, pine scent and orange glow
a numinous pleasure—bathed in nostalgia, it's true,
yet founded, at least for those too young to remember candles,
on the flickering tungsten stem in the painted bulb.
Treats of electricity: reflectors, bubble lamps,
and in the old-fashioned department store displays
those dwarf automatons. Waiting in line
for Santa's Workshop with his fidgety two-year-old,
a man imitates the charming repetitive gestures
of the helpers—this elf picking up a letter,
that one sawing, taking brownies from a smoking toy oven,
playing the violin—small acts that are like ours but not quite,
enticing in their similitude and mechanical regularity
like the set of a dozen prints of the kids posed on Santa's lap.

Things That Go. When Teddy and I leaf through his picture book
at bedtime, browsing among the variations
on cars, trucks, planes and digging machines,
each with its specified function and well-chosen animal crew,
we move through a storehouse of metamorphoses:
the steam shovel wearing a dinosaur grin, a warty
pickle van, a shark car for the freeways
driven by a ferret. If he is ready to jump in
and "make them go," his desire is fueled
not by surprise—he knows what all these are—
but by the familiar, continuously re-animated
and peeking out from behind its protean veil.
A carefully bounded abundance, as in a big store
full of gizmos: the small machines in Gifts,
the larger ones (Appliances) that become part of your house,
or Home Furnishings, where a dozen varieties of ceiling fan
paddle the air. Everywhere the insistent promises
of safe, inexhaustible potential. This is the premise
of the showroom: all the baroque techno-glitter
of the customizing imagination—heady, liberating
(take us for a ride!)—yet always under the hood
the unseen valves and pistons with their steady assuring beat.

The giantism of previous eras appeals.
The train worship of the nineteenth century—
what image is so forceful an analogy
of gritty power? It triumphs over its components,
riding on iron, across wood, above cinders,
converting mere lumps of coal to noise and speed.
Or consider those whirling turbines in thirties movies:
a new sleek cleanness here, a hum instead of a roar,
but the same homage to scale—low-angle shots
of the great dams, jump-suited technicians
on far-off catwalks—and the same child-like pride.
Look, we have made this. It is so much bigger than ourselves,
yet simple. The huge constructions flatter us
because they're intelligible. Like games that effortlessly reduce
history to a deck of cards, a city to a board
we hover over, a famous battalion of soldiers
to toys we can line up across the tabletop.

Here is the classic humanoid fantasy
where all comes clear at last: Mr. Machine.
Inside his see-through casing, the innards buzz
and whirl: lighted tubes down the stiff limbs,
hinges for joints, and a huge red flywheel at the heart.
In him the body is at last comprehensible.
It does its work, comes readily to hand, and responds to commands
with an admirable mechanistic directness.
I think of him as first cousin to The Visible Man,
another relic from the age of transparent polystyrene
who is somehow more disturbing—all those curdled intestines,
chickeny sinews, the slop in the brain pan.
Mr. Machine will have none of this. Angular and clean,
he stands for the dream of limits, perfect
efficiency. The control we have always desired.

Yet this is a nightmare too, as in the ominous
robotic hordes marching down the ramp of the spaceship
or Joey the Mechanical Boy with his hallucinatory matrix
of tubes and wires, his hidden current source
and parodic compulsive jerks. Is it
the final self-control to imagine control by others?
And when the machines do take over (and they will—
remember Jim after the brain tumor, his shaved head
patched with electrodes, the one good eye dulled, transfixed
by the screen), we are put in a kind of womb:
the placenta of IV's and probes, the fluids and currents
brought in and out, all for our own renewal
as we float, a perfect impassive god in the room
in the wing in the larger living tissue of the hospital.

To go inside a machine—not the cartoon version
where the famous talking duck gets caught in the clockworks,
whirling among the figurines, paddled, hammered
in absurd repetition, but the slower cycle
of a commuter. Dan on his weekday morning drive
from Oakland to San Leandro. The machine
incorporates him, in a bubble, in a stream of them
down the freeway. In the semi-transparent cell of the car,
poised behind its throbbing heart, he has at his fingers
control of the sensations of heat and cold, of movement,
sound—a wreath of Vivaldi conjured from the air—
and he is held there as time passes and the other bubbles
follow their daily paths across his windshield
or, one day, in a disaster I never want
to imagine, converge—and the glass, steel and plastic
are forced inside the man inside the car.

Doctors, if they can, will pick out the pieces
while others, in another wing of the hospital,
labor to do the opposite: to fit a machine
inside a man, a new mainspring for the clock of the heart.
It's comforting to see ourselves this way:
the steady beat of the old ticker (aided, if necessary,
by a mylar implant), our decorous grandfather clocks,
our watches where we imagine a face and hands.
The accuracy of these machines consoles—
hence the search for ever more exact
measurements, more regular strokes, cleaner slices
of the obviously dwindling pie till we have moved
from sunlight, sand and water to weights and springs,
the oscillation of a crystal, and at last
atomic decay: relentless decline of the universe
in the precisely calculable losses of its tiniest parts
taken now as a standard for our own running to ground.

There is a place in North Dakota, deep underground,
where a twenty-two-year-old graduate of a military training program
sits on a padded swivel chair in front of a console
intricate and garish as the "Christmas Tree" of a sub, waiting
for a call which he will uncode, check, and answer
with a series of flipped switches.
With his crisp uniform and "Yes, sir!" snap
he seems an anachronism, a stiff cog forgotten
far beneath the transfigured surfaces of foreign policy.
Yet, buried there, he is in control. When the missiles are launched
and later when others score direct hits on the launch site,
we expect him to feel nothing but a dull shudder.
The machines will conduct their unimaginable business
on land, obliterating roads, hospitals, power plants,
the very factories where they were made, while a few men—
our boyish lieutenant, others in subs, the President
soaring in his fabulous getaway plane—
carry out arcane rituals of analysis
and command. This is the vision of invulnerable
continuity: the unhindered clockworks,
Joey needing to be plugged in every day, Dan in his car
on the same old road to his boss and comforting desk.

Though no one actually likes going to work
each morning at a brokerage firm or a typing pool
or an insecticide factory, after we get there
we quickly find our place inside the circuit
of predictable motions and varied impersonal equipment.
Even the task of fitting a pig's intestine
over the sausage dispenser and sealing the stuffed casing
nine times each minute must soothe in its routine
like the insistent ground beat of a primitive mourning chant.
Still it persists, this dream of a life freed from the timeclock,
the machines themselves, benign and miraculously
self-sustaining, lifting us from their service
to some higher realm. What is it? A pastoral fantasy?
Mere regression? Some half-submerged yearning
for the lost grand leisure of the bourgeoisie?
In *The Time Machine*, a heavy-handed fable
from the autumn of British imperialism,
the grimy engines of labor deep in the underworld
boom a rhythmic warning to the bored
and child-like creatures of the surface, who have become
so exquisitely refined they can no longer tell what it means.

Who's in charge here? It's not the fear of chaos
that disturbs us now—the railroad scattering Walden Pond
or London, revolts of our subterranean proles—
but the perfected operation of a system
that has grown, organically it seems, far beyond
our grasp. The black box. The reduction of a bank
to a blank column cranking out bills, the correspondent
expansion and interconnection of the credit card, insurance card,
plasticized driver's license where the traffic cop
finds all we have ever done. We are hauled off,
swept away. Streaming down the freeway
to the identical stores of the malls, the shoppers move
like fluid in tubes, current through the wires, while somewhere else,
in the intricate and busy world of the hospital,
among the vast hidden files, whirring and clicking, the paranoid
poises like a spider at the center of his web.

Refulgent, endlessly exploratory, wiring and reconnecting
its replicating circuits, the brain generates
a tissue of thought. It is a plant, a power grid.
Or a camera obscura, and what it delivers from light
is laced with the maze-like filigree of hypotheses.
When my son sees a new machine and asks,
What makes it run? How does it work? the questions themselves,
and our attempts at answers—phone calls, word searches,
trips to the library to look in the encyclopedia—
fill in the manifold sustaining texture. Order is ubiquitous
and flourishing. Truths flash and vanish in the multiplying
tributaries, the sprouting ganglial nodes.
This is growth, the linking together of an ever finer mesh
to catch particulars of the fluid world. This is also
the obsessive crosshatching that finally blots it all out.

Think of snapshots, the resolute calm of their surfaces:
a man rising in the elevator on his first day back at work,
an interchange at rush hour, the collapse of a house
or a coal mine, a rocket exploding in air.
We can imagine these scenes—and we imagine far worse,
tugging out stasis, moments of escape from the *perpetuum mobile*
of the mind. The engine of thought itself
as a kind of fountain: one great turning wheel
continuously dipping buckets where the water poured
drives its own pouring. When I picture it,
it is not the inevitably slowing clockworks of the whole
that stands out, but the single repeated units:
a basin empty, just filled or filling, a stream
just at the point of entering the pool.
Things that go. If these generated moments
seem pure, willed, pulled out of time
and thus receptive at last to control,
even they are processed, even they
are fretted and scored. Lifted to light, they gleam
with the variegated luster of everything we've made.